*Is There Only
One True
Religion or
Are There Many?*

Is There Only One True Religion or Are There Many?

Schubert M. Ogden

Southern Methodist University Press
Dallas

First edition, 1992

Requests for permission to reproduce material from this work should
be sent to:
Permissions
Southern Methodist University Press
Box 415
Dallas, Texas 75275

Library of Congress Cataloging-in-Publication Data
Ogden, Schubert Miles, 1928–
    Is there only one true religion or are there many? / Schubert M.
Ogden.
        p.   cm.
    Originally delivered as the 1990 Samuel Ferguson Lectures,
University of Manchester (England).
    Includes bibliographical references and index.
    ISBN 0-87074-328-7   ISBN 0-87074-329-5 (pbk.)
    1. Christianity and other religions.   2. Religious pluralism.
I. Title.
BR128.C4033   1992
261.2—dc20   91-52781

To my dialogue partners
in the
International Buddhist-Christian
Theological Encounter Group

CONTENTS

PREFACE

For some time now, the question addressed by this book has been a central question for Christian theology. In fact, discussion of it has already reached the point where it is widely assumed on all sides that the only ways open for answering it are either one of the two older and now challenged options of exclusivism and inclusivism or else the relatively new and challenging option of pluralism. My view is that this assumption is mistaken and that an adequate answer to the question waits upon considering yet a fourth option that has not even been clearly recognized, much less carefully considered. The aim of the book, then, is to reduce this deficit in the previous discussion, by clarifying the issue that the question raises and, therefore, by also taking account of a neglected possibility for answering it beyond the usual options.

That there is such a fourth option is, of course, a matter of logic, of recognizing that the usual ways of answering the question do not exhaust the possibilities that are, in fact, open to a Christian theology of religions. But I have certainly been helped in recognizing this, as in clarifying the underlying issue, by certain traditional theological insights, which readers may well want to bear in mind in following my argument. Particularly important for clarifying the basic concept of a "true religion" is the analogy suggested by the concept of a "true church" in classical Protestant ecclesiology. No less important is the further analogy I employ—here following much recent Roman Catholic theology—in thinking and speaking of Jesus Christ himself as the primal Christian sacrament or means of salvation. Indeed, it is not too much to say, I think, that the kind of representative christology that is fundamental to the fourth option is not likely to carry conviction unless my way of developing this analogy is deemed appropriate.

As for my speaking simply of "the fourth option," I do so only because none of the labels for it that have occurred to me has seemed entirely happy, not because I suppose it to be any less of an ideal type than any of the other three options. As between the extreme contrary positions of exclusivism and pluralism, it is, in a way, closest to pluralism, somewhat as inclusivism, in its way, is closest to exclusivism. But it is also, in a way, close to inclusivism, with which it shares the middle ground between the other two extremes. Perhaps if we could agree to qualify what is here as well as elsewhere distinguished simply as "inclusivism" by speaking instead of "*monistic* inclusivism," we could appropriately speak of the fourth option as "*pluralistic* inclusivism." In any event, the position itself should be clear, and clearly distinguished from all three of the usual options.

Apart from mostly minor changes in style and wording, the four chapters of the book were given in March 1990 as the Samuel Ferguson Lectures at the University of Manchester. To Dean A. O. Dyson and his colleagues in the Faculty of Theology, their students, and all of my other hearers I express my warm thanks both for their cordial reception of my lectures and for the many stimulating discussions occasioned by their comments and questions. I am especially grateful to Dr. David A. Pailin, to whose efforts I owe the invitation to do the lectures and who, with his wife Gwyneth, extended to me the gracious hospitality of their home throughout my stay in Manchester.

Four other persons also deserve special thanks for their contributions to the book: Franklin I. Gamwell, for reading the lectures and giving me the benefit of his criticisms; Betty Manning, for processing all drafts of the lectures as well as of the book; Freddie Goff, for copy editing; and Keith Gregory, for editorial advice and seeing the book through to publication.

True religion is right tempers towards God and man. It is, in two words, gratitude and benevolence: gratitude to our Creator and supreme Benefactor, and benevolence to our fellow-creatures. In other words, it is the loving God with all our heart, and our neighbour as ourselves.

John Wesley

CHAPTER 1

The Challenge of Pluralism

Among the many ways of formulating the Christian claim is to assert that the Christian religion is the true religion. In fact, throughout most of their history, Christians have typically asserted or implied that the Christian religion is the only true religion. But if this assertion may be fairly taken as typical of Christian witness, it has also long been more or less problematic in Christian theology—and for theologians charged with the responsibility of critically reflecting on this witness.

One thinks, for instance, of what the aged Augustine, determined to clarify his earlier writings and to retract any errors in them, had to say about his treatise, "Of True Religion":

> Again, in the same chapter, I said "That is the Christian religion in our times, which to know and follow is most sure and certain salvation." I was speaking of the name here, and not of the thing so named. For what is now called the Christian religion existed of

old and was never absent from the beginning of the human race until Christ came in the flesh. Then true religion which already existed began to be called Christian. After the resurrection and ascension of Christ into heaven, the apostles began to preach him and many believed, and the disciples were first called Christian in Antioch, as it is written. When I said, "This is the Christian religion in our times," I did not mean that it had not existed in former times, but that it received that name later. (Augustine, 218f.)

Just what Augustine's clarification or retraction comes to may not be entirely certain. But it makes clear enough that he was no longer willing to endorse any simple identification of the true religion with the Christian religion such as many Christians both before and since have asserted or implied in advancing the Christian claim.

One generalization that can be safely made about Christian theologians today is that more and more of them are evidencing the same unwillingness. Far from endorsing the claim that the Christian religion is the only true religion, they are increasingly asking whether this can possibly be a valid Christian claim. The principal reason for this is that an ever larger number not only of theologians but of Christians generally are now making or implying another very different, indeed contrary, claim. According to them, the Christian religion is but one of many religions, or logically comparable ways of understanding human existence, some if not all of which are as true as Christianity. Thus, from the standpoint of Christians and theologians who make or imply this contrary claim, the Christian religion may indeed be the true religion, but only in the sense in which the same may be said of other religions or comparable ways of existing as human beings. Because of this insistence that there are many true religions rather than one, the name by which this claim has now come to be generally known is "pluralism." And it is because of pluralism in this sense that Christian theologians today have increasingly had to ask whether the monism typical of most Christian tradition can any longer be accepted as valid.

Of course, in some senses religious pluralism is nothing new. If the word "pluralism" is understood, as it often is, simply as a synonym for the word "plurality," religious pluralism has always existed, since there has always been a plurality of religions in the world in which Christians have had to bear their witness and reflect theologically on the validity of their claims in doing so. Until quite recently, however, the many religions, like the many cultures with which they are of a piece, lived for the most part in mutual isolation. Only with the revolutions of the recent past, especially the technological revolution in transportation and communication, has this isolation finally been broken through, to the point where the many religions and cultures are now compelled to live with one another as next-door neighbors in a single global village. It is this enforced proximity of each religion and culture to every other that is the really new thing about religious and cultural plurality in our situation today.

On the other hand, the word "pluralism" is also properly understood to mean not simply the state or condition of plurality, but the belief or doctrine that affirms and advocates plurality as a good thing (cf. Ogden 1983). And in this sense, too, religious pluralism is not entirely new. At least since the Renaissance, theologians have spoken, in Nicholas of Cusa's words, of "one faith in the diversity of religions"; and already at the beginning of the nineteenth century, in the theology of Friedrich Schleiermacher, there was a clean break with the claim that Christianity is the only true religion. But what does seem to be new to our century, especially the second half of it, is the growing number of Christians and theologians who are proposing a pluralistic theology of religions. Out of their experiences of religious plurality, and thus a keener and more informed sense both of the strengths of other religious traditions and of the weaknesses of their own, they have come to affirm and advocate such plurality as a good thing—not in spite of their Christian commitment, but because of it. More and more of them are religious pluralists precisely as Christians and theologians; and this is why the challenge they pose to Christian witness and theology is new, and importantly new at that.

My concern as a theologian and in this book is to address the question that this challenge has now made theologically central: Is there only one true religion, or are there many? Clearly, if the proponents of religious pluralism are correct, the older options between which Christians and theologians have typically chosen in answering this question cannot be theologically valid insofar as they alike imply religious monism in asserting that there is only one true religion. But the issue for theology is whether religious pluralists are right about this and whether their new option can itself be theologically validated, or whether, on the contrary, their assertion that there are many true religions is, in its way, problematic enough that it, too, is vulnerable to the challenge of some more adequate option.

This is the issue that I hope to clarify, if hardly settle, in subsequent chapters. Meanwhile, we need to look more closely at the challenge of pluralism to the older options for answering our central question. In order to do this, I want, first of all, to consider in some detail the question itself: the terms in which it is formulated and certain of their presuppositions and implications, as I understand them.

The basic term here, of course, is "religion," and the difficulties involved in satisfactorily defining it are notorious. Even so, we cannot expect a clear answer to the question of whether there is only one true religion or rather many without clarifying how we are using "religion" in asking it. Without claiming, then, to give a wholly satisfactory definition of the term, I offer the following clarification of its meaning in the present inquiry.

By "religion" I understand the primary form of culture in terms of which we human beings explicitly ask and answer the existential question of the meaning of ultimate reality for us. Presupposed by this summary clarification is, first of all and most fundamentally, that among the questions that we human beings find ourselves typically asking and answering is what I call "the existential question."

To be human is not only to exist together with others, both human and nonhuman, but also to understand oneself and others and reality generally and, within limits, to be responsible for them. At the root of this responsibility is the distinctive freedom that is ours in consequence of our capacity for understanding both ourselves and others and the encompassing whole of reality of which we are all parts. Unlike other animals whose overall course of life is largely determined by species-specific instincts, we are "instinct poor." Not only the details of our lives but even their overall pattern as authentically human remain undecided by our membership in the human species and are left to our own freedom and responsibility to decide. To be sure, the freedom of any one of us as an individual is in a way preempted by the decisions already made by those who have gone before us in the particular society and culture into which we are born or in which it is given to us to become human. But while none of us can be socialized and acculturated without internalizing some already decided understanding of human existence, the very process of internalization serves to develop our capacity for understanding and, therefore, for questioning the validity of our cultural inheritance. In other words, we acquire the ability to ask the existential question of how we are to understand ourselves and others in relation to the whole if ours is to be an authentic human existence.

Underlying this question as its "basic supposition" is the faith that there is such an authentic self-understanding—that the ultimate reality of one's own existence together with others in the whole is

question of the meaning of ultimate reality for us. This means, first of all, that the reality about which it asks is the ultimate reality of our own existence in relation to others and the whole. I speak of this reality as "ultimate" on the assumption that by the term "reality" used without qualification, we mean, in William James's words, "what we in some way find ourselves obliged to take account of" (James, 101). Clearly, whatever else we may or may not find ourselves obliged to take account of, we can never fail to take account somehow of ourselves, others, and the whole to which we all belong. In this sense, the threefold reality of our existence simply as such is the ultimate reality that we all have to allow for in leading our own individual lives. But if this reality is what the existential question asks about, the second thing to note is how it does this—namely, by asking about this reality, not in its structure in itself, but in its meaning for us. This implies that in asking about ultimate reality, the existential question asks, at one and the same time, about our authentic self-understanding, about the understanding of ourselves in relation to others and the whole that is appropriate to, or authorized by, this ultimate reality itself.

Thus, by its very nature, the existential question is a single question having two closely related and yet clearly distinguishable aspects. In one of these aspects, it asks about the ultimate reality of our own existence in relation to others and the whole. This I distinguish as its *metaphysical* aspect, because, while it is distinct from metaphysics proper in asking about this ultimate reality in its meaning for us rather than in its structure in itself, it is nonetheless closely related to metaphysics in that any answer to it necessarily has metaphysical implications. Unless ultimate reality in itself has one structure rather than another, it cannot have the meaning for us that a specific religion represents it as having. In its other aspect, which I distinguish as *ethical,* the existential question asks about our authentic self-understanding. Thus, while it is distinct from ethics proper in asking how we are to understand ourselves rather than how we are to act and what we are to do, it is nonetheless closely related to ethics in that any answer to it necessarily has ethical implications. Unless acting in one way rather than another is how we ought to act in relation to others, ultimate reality cannot authorize the understanding of our existence that a specific religion represents it as authorizing.

This means, of course, that, by the very nature of the existential question, there are also two main aspects to the procedures appropriate to determining the truth of specific religious answers to it. Broadly speaking, we may say that a specific answer is true insofar as it so responds to the question as to solve the problem that all religions exist to solve— the problem, namely, of making sense somehow of our basic faith in the meaning of life, given the facts of life as we actually experience it. But whether, or to what extent, a specific religious answer is capable of doing this can be determined only by verifying its necessary implications, ethical as well as metaphysical. If it is true, its implications also must be true; and unless they can be verified by procedures appropriate to ethical and metaphysical claims respectively, it cannot be verified, either.

To recognize this is to understand the difficulties of validating claims to religious truth. As compared with science and technology, where there is extensive agreement concerning appropriate procedures of verification, ethics and metaphysics are both profoundly controversial fields of inquiry, even at the level of the principles and procedures by which true claims are to be distinguished from false. In fact, there is not even agreement about the proper analysis of metaphysical and ethical utterances, which some philosophers construe as having a noncognitive kind of meaning that obviates even asking about their truth or falsity. Small wonder, then, that one of the standing temptations of religious believers is to try to find some way of avoiding the difficulties of validating their claims, whether by simply deducing their truth from some alleged divine revelation or by construing them as matters of faith, whose truth supposedly cannot and need not be validated. But only a little reflection confirms the futility of all such moves, especially in a situation such as ours today, in which the plurality of religious claims is an ever-present fact of life. Unless one is prepared to allow that one's claim to religious truth is something very different from the kind of cognitive claim that it gives every appearance of being, one is left either with reneging on the promise implied in making the claim or with redeeming its validity in a non-question-begging way by the only procedures appropriate to doing so. Consequently, there is no avoiding the difficulties of validating religious claims if one is to be responsible in making them as claims to truth. By the very logic of such claims, the only way to validate them is to verify their necessary implications both metaphysical and ethical by the same procedures that would be appropriate for any other claims of the same logical types.

This is not to say that any specific religious answer can be deduced simply from a true metaphysics and a true ethics, taken either singly or together. Any religion, as we have seen, is more than self-understanding insofar as it is also the primary "cultural system" through which a certain understanding of existence is explicitly represented as authentic. Therefore, while the truth of its self-understanding, insofar as it is true, must indeed be implied by a true metaphysics and a true ethics, it itself as a particular way of conceiving and symbolizing its self-understanding is irreducibly historical. As such, it is simply given—a datum for metaphysics and ethics rather than a deduction from them. And this means that validating its claim to truth also always involves certain properly historical and hermeneutical procedures.

I should perhaps also make clear that I in no way suppose that one must first have a true metaphysics and a true ethics before one can determine whether or not a specific religion is true. To argue, as I have, that determining the truth of a religion logically requires verifying its necessary implications for both belief and action does not imply that one must already be in possession of metaphysical and ethical truth when one undertakes to verify them. On the contrary, it is entirely possible that in following the procedures requisite to their verification, one will not only determine the truth of the religion implying them, but will also determine the falsity of a metaphysics or an ethics that one previously took to be true.

To sum up, then, the term "true religion" refers to one or more specific religions whose claim to be formally true, and hence the norm for determining all other true religion, is a valid claim, as determined by the procedures of verification that have just been indicated. I stress the words "one or more" here because in other things that I have written on this subject I have sometimes failed to express myself with sufficient care. Thus, in one such passage, I inferred from the statement that "religion never exists in general, . . . but always only as *a* religion" that "even the true religion, if there be such a thing, could not be identified with religion in general or simply as such. It could only be one particular religion among others distinguished from all the rest solely by the unique adequacy with which its particular concepts and symbols answered to the need that each religion exists to meet" (Ogden 1986, 110). No doubt, the main point of this inference was to underscore my claim that religion is like any other form of culture in never existing in general but always only in particular. But the way in which I made this point unfortunately suggests that, by the very meaning of the term, there could be only one true religion. And if this were so we could not ask our central question except by begging it. This, however, I in no way want to suggest; and so I emphasize that the term "true religion," as I have tried to clarify its meaning, fully allows for the possibility that there is more than one specific religion whose claim to be formally true is a valid claim.

Of course, there is another important question that is, in fact, begged by asking, Is there only one true religion, or are there many? The supposition of this question is that either some religion is or some religions are formally true; and the point of asking it is to decide which of these two possibilities is really the case. But to suppose that either is the case is to take neither of two other positions, both of which are also possibilities from a purely logical point of view (cf. Küng, 278–85).

Thus it is not to take the position, first of all, that *no* religion is the true religion. Indeed, as the logical contradictory of this position, the supposition that we make simply in asking our question already rules it out as necessarily false. This may not seem unreasonable, considering that ours, after all, is a theological inquiry occasioned by the challenge of pluralism to the monistic claim that there is only one true religion. But thus to suppose that not all religions are false because one or more religions are true is clearly to beg a question to which others have given a contradictory answer only after offering relevant evidence and argument to support it. Often enough, to be sure, the convincingness of their case has depended upon some substantive definition of "religion" much narrower and more exclusive than the strictly functional understanding that I have argued for here. Given this broader, more inclusive understanding, it is certainly not obvious that no

CHAPTER 2

The Case against Exclusivism

In Chapter 1, I attempted to clarify the challenge of pluralism to the claim typical of much Christian witness, that Christianity is the only true religion. To this end, I considered in some detail the question that this challenge has now made theologically central and that I propose to address in this book: Is there only one true religion, or are there many? Pluralists, I argued, typically take the second position on this question insofar as they hold not only that there *can be* many true religions but that there actually *are*. They thus contend that the claim of more than one specific religion to be formally true, and, therefore, the norm for determining any other true religion, is a valid claim.

The issue before us in this and succeeding chapters is the correctness of this contention. To clarify this issue, I want to begin by looking more closely at the first position on our question against which the challenge of pluralism is directed.

Up to this point, I have spoken of this position simply as "religious monism" so as to contrast it explicitly and directly with religious pluralism. But in actual fact, pluralism is a challenge not merely to one but to two ways of answering our question, which are significantly different, even though they alike claim that the Christian religion is the only true religion. Therefore, if we are to clarify the issue before us, we need to take account of both of these other options and to understand the difference as well as the similarity between their two answers.

We noted at the beginning of the first chapter that Christians have typically claimed that the Christian religion alone is the true religion. This they have claimed for the very good reason that, from their standpoint, no other religion even can be true in the same sense in which this can be said of Christianity. Although all religions make or imply the claim to be formally true, and hence normative for determining all other religious truth, the only religion whose claim to this effect can possibly be valid is the religion established by God in the unique saving event of Jesus Christ. Since only the Christian religion can be said to be thus established, it alone can validly claim to be the formally true religion.

For many, if not most, Christians this kind of religious monism has been understood exclusivistically in that they have denied the possibility of participating in the true religion, and thus obtaining salvation, to any and all non-Christians. The classical formula for such exclusivism is the dictum that goes back to the Latin church father Cyprian: *extra ecclesiam nulla salus* — "outside of the church there is no salvation." Some interpreters have held that this formula strictly applies only to the Roman Catholic form of exclusivism, since Protestant exclusivists have typically claimed instead that there is no salvation outside of Christianity (Hick and Knitter, 16f.). But this seems to me to be a misleading way of stating the relevant difference, since in both cases salvation is possible only in and through the visible church and its proclamation. In the case of Roman Catholics, however, who have classically identified the visible church with their own institutional church, exclusivism has meant that there is no salvation, because no participation in the true religion, outside of the Church of Rome. In the case of Protestants, by contrast, exclusivism has meant that no one could expect to belong to the invisible church of the chosen except by belonging to the visible church of the called through membership in some true institutional church. In both cases, exclusivism is the option that not only asserts Christianity to be the only true religion, but also holds that Christians alone, as participants in this religion through their membership in the visible church, obtain the salvation that God established it to mediate.

From late antiquity through the nineteenth century, Christians in the West typically exercised this option of exclusivism in one or the other of its different forms. Throughout this period, they widely believed that Christianity was destined to spread throughout the world, eventually displacing all of the other non-Christian religions; and firm in this belief, they increasingly gave themselves to the missionary outreach that led to modern Christian expansion. But exclusivism has never been the only option open to Christians; and since roughly World War I, which in this as in other ways was the real end of the nineteenth century, there has been a growing movement away from it. This has happened in part, no doubt, because of increasing knowledge, as well as extensive first-hand experience, of other religious and cultural traditions, especially of the other axial religions. But ever since World War II and the breakup of the European colonial empires in Africa and Asia, many Christians have also become more and more aware of the negative impact of exclusivism on the non-Christian majority of the world's population. Having served only too often to sanction the acquisitiveness and violence of Western imperialism, exclusivistic claims are now seen to be profoundly ambiguous if not yet totally discredited.

The upshot is that for some three-quarters of a century, and increasingly during the last thirty years or so, Christians have been moving away from traditional exclusivism toward a more inclusivistic way of claiming that theirs is the only true religion. To a considerable extent, this has happened by their retrieving an alternative theological tradition that, ever since the New Testament, has made the possibility of salvation independent of participation in the true religion through membership in the visible church. In any case, clear evidences of the emergence of such inclusivism are to be seen on the Roman Catholic side in the theological developments leading up to the Second Vatican Council and its official statements about the church and the relation of the church to non-Christian religions; and on the Protestant and Orthodox side in the parallel developments taking place in the World Council of Churches Subunit on Dialogue with People of Living Faiths and Ideologies.

If we ignore certain differences in nuance and formulation, these developments have all led to a way of answering our question that is significantly different from that of exclusivism. According to this answer, the possibility of salvation uniquely constituted by the event of Jesus Christ is somehow made available to each and every human being without exception and, therefore, is exclusive of no one unless she or he excludes her- or himself from its effect by a free and responsible decision to reject it. Since salvation itself is thus universally possible, and in this sense is all-inclusive, there is also the possibility of all religions being more or less substantially true insofar as this salvation becomes effective in human beings, thereby transforming their self-objectification in the explicit forms of religion as well as in culture generally. Thus not only can all individuals be saved by the salvation constituted by Christ, but all religions also can be more or less valid means of this salvation to those who either are not or cannot become members of the visible church. At the same time, Christian inclusivists continue to maintain that Christianity alone can be the formally true religion, since it alone is the religion established by God in the unique saving event of Jesus Christ and, therefore, alone expresses normatively the religious truth that is represented at best fragmentarily and inadequately in all other religious ways. Thus, while, according to Christian inclusivism, non-Christians can indeed be saved because or insofar as they accept Christ's salvation as it is made available to them anonymously and unknowingly and through the means of their own religions, Christians alone are related to the same salvation explicitly and knowingly in the way which it is the abiding mission of the visible church to bring about in the life of each and every person.

Notwithstanding its significant difference from exclusivism, then, inclusivism is, in its way, monistic rather than pluralistic in its understanding of true religion. For it, too, there not only is but can be only one true religion, in the sense that Christianity alone can validly claim to be formally true. Recognizing this, one of its most astute critics, John Hick, dismisses it as anomalous—"like the anomaly of accepting the Copernican revolution in astronomy, in which the earth ceased to be regarded as the center of the universe and was seen instead as one of the planets circling the sun, but still insisting that the sun's life-giving rays can reach the other planets only by first being reflected from the earth!" (Hick and Knitter, 23).

We will return to a consideration of inclusivism in later chapters, especially the last. Meanwhile, having distinguished it from exclusivism, we have now taken account of all three of the usual options for answering our central question. In addition to the relatively new and challenging option of pluralism, there are the two older options of exclusivism and inclusivism, both of which are now being challenged in their monistic answers to the question.

Not surprisingly, pluralists are particularly keen to distinguish their position from that of inclusivists, which they consider anomalous and unstable. In their view, either inclusivists must fall back on the exclusivism from which they have turned away, or else they must push ahead to the pluralism that alone offers a consistent alternative. For all of their sharp criticism of inclusivism, however, pluralists are more than willing to accept its help in overthrowing the common enemy of exclusivism. In fact, the combined opposition that their alliance with inclusivists makes possible means that exclusivism has become an increasingly embattled position. Even so, the theological issue is whether this development is justified. Does exclusivism deserve to be overthrown? How strong is the case against it?

My judgment is that the case against it is exceptionally strong—as strong, in fact, as a theological case is likely to be. But an adequate defense of this judgment, such as I shall attempt in this chapter, requires that we first pay attention to what has to be done to make a theological case. The benefits of attending to this, of course, are not limited to the largely critical case to be made in this chapter, but also extend to the argument of the book generally, in its more constructive as well as its more critical aspects.

I begin by recalling a reference made in passing in Chapter 1 to what I distinguished as theology in the generic sense of the word. Theology in this sense, I said, is a secondary form of culture consisting in critical reflection on the validity claims of some specific religion. Whereas religion as a primary form of culture involves making or implying certain claims to validity, theology as a secondary form of culture involves critically validating or invalidating these same claims. Theology is not alone in doing this, of course, since philosophy, also, involves critically reflecting on the claims of religion, along with those of so-called secular forms of praxis and culture. But what distinguishes theology in the generic sense from philosophy, including what I refer to as "philosophical theology," is that it is constituted as such by critical reflection on the validity claims of this or that specific religion (cf. Ogden 1986, 69–93, 121–33). This means that theology in the specific sense of Christian theology, which is our immediate concern here, neither would nor could exist at all but for the prior existence of the Christian religion, whose claims to validity it is constituted to validate.

The problem with putting it this way, however, is that it is much too abstract. The claims in question are not really made or implied by the Christian religion, but by concrete human beings, as groups and as individuals, who think and speak of themselves as Christians in making or implying them. Consequently, the concrete data of Christian theological reflection are provided by the religious praxis, or, as I like to call it, the "witness," of all of these human beings who profess to be Christians.

Analysis discloses, I maintain, that any instance of such Christian witness expresses or implies two distinctive claims to validity. On the one hand, it claims to be adequate to its content and, therefore, substantially if not formally true; on the other hand, it claims to be fitting to its situation. Actually, Christian witness makes or implies three claims, since its claim to be adequate to its content and hence also true itself involves two further claims: first, that what is thought, said, or done in bearing the witness is appropriate to Jesus Christ; and second, that it is credible to human existence. In the broadest sense, then, Christian theology as critical reflection on the claims to validity expressed or implied by Christian witness consists in critically validating all three of these claims: to be adequate to its content and, therefore, appropriate and credible, and to be fitting to its situation.

But the words "Christian theology" are also commonly used in a narrower sense to refer to the particular discipline of Christian systematic theology, rather than to the field of Christian theology as a whole. Here, again, our immediate concern warrants our focusing on Christian theology in this narrower sense of the words. This means that, in the sense intended here, theology consists in critically validating the claim of Christian witness to be adequate to its content, the task of validating the other claim of witness to be fitting to its situation being the proper task of Christian practical theology. What has to be done, then, to make the theological case against exclusivism that I propose to make is to invalidate its claim to be adequate to its content and, therefore, substantially true; and this entails, of course, invalidating its two further claims to be appropriate to Jesus Christ and credible to human existence.

I underscore that making the case against exclusivism entails invalidating both of these further claims. There is no question that traditional Christian exclusivism has long since ceased to be plausible, much less credible, to many men and women both within the church and outside of it. On this ground alone, then, it is widely rejected as an untenable position, and Christian theologians commonly assume that it must at all costs be abandoned. But this, in my opinion, is to follow a defective theological procedure, and this would be so even if what is widely held to be incredible were to be critically invalidated as exactly that. Pending the critical reflection necessary to determine otherwise, one must allow, at least as a possibility, that Christian exclusivism's other claim to be appropriate to Jesus Christ could be critically validated. In that event, of course, invalidating its claim to be credible would invalidate the constitutive assertion of Christian witness itself, since Jesus could not then be the decisive re-presentation of the truth about human existence that Christians attest him to be in asserting him to be the Christ. But concern to avoid this eventuality cannot excuse following a procedure in theology that is in principle faulty. On the contrary, the only way to make a theological case against exclusivism is to invalidate both of its claims—its claim to be appropriate to Jesus Christ as well as its claim to be credible to human existence.

To invalidate either claim naturally requires employing relevant criteria or norms. In the case of the claim to be credible, the relevant criteria are common human experience and reason. If exclusivism is worthy of being believed, it can only be because it somehow has the support of what any human being can experience and understand. If, on the other hand, exclusivism is incredible, this must be because it is lacking in such support— whether because experience and reason clearly tell against it or simply because they are not sufficient to bear it out. To invalidate its claim to be credible is to show one or the other of these possibilities to be the actual situation.

In the case of its claim to be appropriate, the relevant criteria or norms are quite different. Like other religious traditions, the Christian tradition is heterogeneous in composition insofar as, through special acts of self-definition, it has specified certain of its elements as normative for some or all of the others. Thus, whether or not a given witness or theology is appropriate to Jesus Christ must be determined by whether or not it is in substantial agreement with these normative elements, and, ultimately, with *the* formal norm or canon with which all other elements must substantially agree.

The difficulty in determining this, however, is that there has never been complete agreement among Christians about what elements are to count as formally normative, either in fact or in principle. To be sure, they have generally agreed during most of their history that it is the original and originating witness of the apostles that is in principle formally normative. But aside from the fact, evidenced by the history of the canon, that they have always disagreed about just what witness or witnesses can be validated as apostolic, exactly what apostolicity itself is to mean even as a principle has also been profoundly controversial. Thus, while Protestants, Roman Catholics, and Orthodox have all traditionally accepted the same apostolic principle, they have understood it in sharply different ways—Protestants appealing to "scripture alone" as apostolic, Roman Catholics and Orthodox invoking alternative understandings of "scripture and tradition" as the real meaning of apostolicity. And as if this were not enough, the revisionary forms of witness and theology that have emerged in modern Christian history have challenged the very principle of apostolicity itself, replacing appeal to it with appeal to the so-called historical Jesus as the real principle of formally normative witness.

This is not the place, obviously, to try to eliminate this difficulty. There are simply different views on what is to count as formally normative both in principle and in fact, and none of these views is completely free of more or less serious problems. All I can do, therefore, is briefly summarize my own view on the question, and refer to discussions I have provided elsewhere that more amply explain and defend it (see, for example, Ogden 1982, 96–105; 1986, 45–68).

My view is that the answer to the question classically given in the Protestant formula, *sola scriptura*—"scripture alone"—is sound in principle even though it is no longer tenable in fact. It is sound in principle because there are the very best of reasons for acknowledging the unique authority of the original and originating witness of the apostles. With the emergence of their witness, although not before, the

Christian religion was definitively established; and it is solely through their witness, finally, that all others who have come to participate in this religion have been authorized to do so. Insofar, then, as the Protestant scriptural principle acknowledges the sole primary authority of the apostolic witness, it is and remains entirely sound. But what is no longer tenable is its identification of scripture, or the New Testament, as in fact apostolic witness. Given the methods and results of historical knowledge now available to us, we know that not a single New Testament writing can be apostolic in the sense of original and originating Christian witness, since their authors all make use of other Christian witnesses, oral and/or written, earlier than themselves. Consequently, to apply the apostolic principle today, in the light of such knowledge, is perforce to abandon the scriptural principle as such, in its classical Protestant form. It is to locate what is formally normative in fact, not in the canon of scripture, or in some "canon *within* the canon," but in a canon *before* the canon—specifically, in the earliest stratum of Christian witness now accessible to us through the methods and results of our own historical knowledge, which is all that we can responsibly identify as apostolic witness.

In my view, then, whether or not a given witness or theology is appropriate to Jesus Christ must be determined, finally, by whether or not it is in substantial agreement with this earliest accessible stratum of Christian witness. Thus, if exclusivism validly claims to be appropriate, it can only be because it substantially agrees with this witness. If, on the other hand, the claim of exclusivism is to be invalidated, this can be done only by showing its disagreement with the very substance of this witness, which is to say, the understanding of existence of which the witness as such is the formally normative formulation.

So much, then, for what has to be done to make the case against exclusivism. I now want to develop what I take to be the decisive objections against it. To this end, I shall first consider somewhat more closely just what it is that exclusivists today typically hold. I stress that it is with a typical position that my argument is concerned and that what I mean by exclusivists is simply Christians or theologians who hold this type of position, to whatever extent they in fact do so.

According to the presuppositions of exclusivism, the predicament of human beings universally is a consequence of their sin, understood not merely as moral transgression, which is rather the result of sin, but as the deeper refusal of a human being to live, finally, in radical dependence upon God, solely by God's grace. Thus, while each and every person is created good and in God's own image, all human beings so misuse their freedom as to sin in this deeper sense of the word. In thus deciding for existence in sin, however, they forfeit their original possibility of existence in faith; and they have no prospect of ever actualizing this possibility unless God acts preveniently to restore it to them. But it is just this that God has in fact done in sending Jesus Christ and in thereby establishing the visible church with its proclamation of salvation.

Anyone who is encountered by this proclamation is once again restored to the possibility of faith, sin notwithstanding; and actualization of this possibility through acceptance of the proclamation is salvation from sin and liberation from the human predicament.

It is just as true, however, that everyone else remains trapped in this predicament and without prospect of salvation. And this is the great difficulty; for it means, in effect, that the human predicament of some persons is radically different from that of others. Since the coming of Jesus Christ and the establishment of the Christian proclamation are events occurring at a particular time and place in history, only persons living after these events and somehow capable of being encountered by the proclamation have any possibility of being saved from their sin. But, then, the predicament of all other persons is not simply a consequence of their sin, in the sense of something for which they themselves, through the misuse of their freedom, are each individually responsible; it is also the predicament of having unfortunately been born at the wrong time or place, a matter of fate rather than freedom, in no way their own responsibility.

To be sure, in the classical formulations of exclusivism in orthodox theology, this difficulty is considerably mitigated or qualified by a larger context of other theological claims. Thus exclusivists have traditionally been able to believe that the Christian proclamation of Jesus Christ was already present prophetically in the Hebrew scriptures, and hence to everyone included in the old covenant.

Furthermore, it is a traditional teaching going all the way back to the church fathers that the gospel was first proclaimed to Adam and Eve through the so-called proto-evangelium of Gen. 3:15 and in this way was already made available to the whole human race. Finally, exclusivists have always been able to qualify their position by allowing for extraordinary acts of God through which individuals are given the possibility of salvation otherwise than through the ordinary means thereof that God has established in the visible church and its word and sacraments. But all of these other claims have long since ceased to provide a credible context for Christian exclusivism. Historical-critical study of scripture has undercut any claim that Jesus Christ was already proclaimed prophetically in the Hebrew scriptures. It has made clear, in fact, that this claim is the classic case of Christians in the present using such methods as are available to them for interpreting their past as will yield what is now called, by a revealing phrase, "usable tradition." Still less plausible is any notion that the gospel was already proclaimed figuratively to Adam and Eve, so that all of their descendants originally had the possibility of faith restored to them. Such allegorical interpretation is totally discredited, and there is no evidence whatever of the gospel's ever having been universally disseminated to all members of the human race. As for special saving acts of God, they are on the face of it arbitrary and ad hoc and are so far from providing any solution to the problem as to be simply another case of it.

Add to this, then, that the sciences continue to date the origins of human life ever earlier in the history of our planet, and it is clear that exclusivists today face a difficult choice. Either they must so alter their original position that only Christians are saved as to allow for the salvation also of non-Christians, at least of participants in God's covenant with Israel and, possibly, of persons included in other dispensations of God's grace; or else they can maintain their original position, but only by conceding that even those included in the old covenant, along with the overwhelming majority of the human race, could not possibly have been saved. Through no fault of their own, all but a tiny minority of the human beings who have lived and died have been allowed to remain in their sin, with despair of salvation the only realistic attitude to their condition.

Assuming now that this is the typical position of Christian exclusivists, I want to object, first of all, that it cannot be validated as credible in terms of common human experience and reason. In principle, at least, one could be so encountered by the Christian proclamation as to experience it as making one's salvation possible, somewhat in the way in which one can experience the words or deeds of another person as enabling one to exist with a new sense of confidence and hope for the future, notwithstanding one's faults in the past. On the basis of this experience, then, one could also make or imply the kind of assertion about the decisive significance of Jesus Christ for salvation that Christians have been wont to make or imply, beginning with the formally normative witness of the apostles. Moreover, this assertion would very definitely imply an exclusivistic claim of sorts—that even as Jesus Christ is the one through whom God decisively acts to save, so the only God who saves is the one who acts decisively through Jesus Christ. Whether or not this claim were true, then, could be determined, again, at least in principle, by validating its necessary implications for both belief and action by following appropriate procedures of metaphysical and ethical verification. But nothing that even a Christian could experience would warrant holding that the way in which she or he and other Christians have been given the possibility of salvation is the only way in which it has been or can be given. In fact, even if one could say that Christianity is the only religion that can be formally true, because it alone is established by God in the unique saving event of Jesus Christ, one would still have no basis for saying that Christians alone are saved or that the possibility of salvation is given only by the Christian proclamation. And if one did say it, there would be no way, even in principle, of ever verifying it in terms of common human experience and reason, since no human experience could show that God has not given or cannot give the possibility of salvation in some other way.

In short, if exclusivism has any basis in experience at all, it can only be in divine experience, not in human. God alone could experience the Christian proclamation as the only way, or, at least, the only ordinary way, in which God gives men and women the possibility of salvation. But this means that exclusivism is indeed an incredible theological position, since human experience and reason are insufficient to support it. Even if it were true, it could not be shown to be so in the only terms that would warrant our accepting it as worthy of belief.

We saw earlier that the same objection would need to be made to the Christian witness itself if exclusivism could make good its further claim to be appropriate to Jesus Christ. But if I am right, this claim, also, is invalid, and this is the second decisive objection against the exclusivistic answer to our question. Far from being appropriate to Jesus Christ, it is, in fact, deeply inappropriate to him in denying the understanding of God that he necessarily implies in explicitly authorizing Christian faith. Consider the following argument.

According to the analysis of religion developed in Chapter 1, specifically Christian faith, like any other, may be characterized purely formally as an explicit self-understanding, or understanding of one's existence in relation to others and the whole. As such, however, it is the only explicit self-understanding decisively authorized by Jesus whom Christians assert to be the Christ, the point of their assertion being that it is at one and the same time the very self-understanding implicitly authorized as the authentic understanding of human existence by ultimate reality itself in its meaning for us. If we ask, then, for the material content of this self-understanding, the only appropriate answer, judging from the formally normative witness of the apostles, is that it is an understanding of ourselves and all others as alike the objects of God's all-embracing love. It is precisely as himself the explicit gift and demand of God's love that Jesus is represented in this earliest witness; and to understand oneself as one is given and called to do decisively through him is to understand oneself as both loved by God and claimed by God's love.

Essential to this self-understanding is a distinctive double structure: it is both trust in God's love alone for the ultimate meaning of our lives and loyalty to God's love as the only final cause that our lives, and all lives, are intended to serve. Although in both aspects, faith is a human response to God's love, but for which it would not be possible, its first aspect of trust is relatively more passive, while its second aspect of loyalty is relatively more active. Moreover, the priority of the first and more passive aspect of trust to the second and more active aspect of loyalty is irreversible. It is only through first accepting God's love in trust that we become sufficiently free from ourselves and all others to be truly loyal to God's cause. It is just as true, however, that if we truly trust in God's love, we cannot fail to live in loyalty to it. Therefore, while this second aspect of faith is and must be strictly posterior to the first, there is nevertheless but one faith with two aspects, each of which necessarily implies the other.

To be loyal to God's love, however, is to be loyal not only to God but also to all to whom God is loyal; and this means, of course, everyone, all others as well as ourselves. But to be loyal to another necessarily involves—if, indeed, it is not simply another word for—loving the other, in the sense of so accepting the other as to take account of the other's interests and then acting toward the other on the basis of such acceptance. So it is that the faith that can originate only by our trusting in God's prevenient love for all of us can eventuate only in our returning love for God and, in God, for all whom God loves.

But if the meaning of God for us is the gift and demand of unbounded love that authorizes trust in this love and loyalty to its cause as our authentic self-understanding, the strictly ultimate reality called "God" has to have a unique structure in itself. Just as it must be inclusive both of self and of all others and, therefore, completely universal in scope and function, so it must also be genuinely individual in being a single center of interaction, both acting on and being acted on by itself and all others. In all ordinary cases, of course, universality and individuality are distinguishing properties, the most universal things being the least individual, and vice versa. But if the kind of trust in God's love and loyalty to its cause that are Christian faith are, in fact, authorized by ultimate reality in its meaning for us, then the structure of this reality in itself, in its strictly ultimate aspect, must be as individual as it is universal, or as universal as it is individual, and hence the one great exception to the rule by which individuals and universals are otherwise distinguished.

The same conclusion follows from the demand of God's love as summarized in the commandments that we shall love the Lord our God with the whole of our being and that we shall love our neighbors as ourselves. Clearly, if it is God whom we are to love with all of our powers, God must be one individual distinct from all others whose interests we can take account of and act to realize. At the same time, if we are also to accept our neighbors as ourselves and act so as to realize all of their interests, even while all of our powers are to be exercised in our love for God, God must also be completely universal in that there can be no interest either of ourselves or of our neighbors that is not somehow included in God's interests.

The God implied by love for God as well as by faith in God, then, cannot be simply one individual among others but must be the one and only completely universal individual. This means that the strictly ultimate whole of reality that we experience as necessary in contrast to the radical contingency both of ourselves and all others must also be distinctively dipolar in its essential structure. It belongs to the very concept of an individual, and hence to any individual whatever, that it be a center of interaction that both acts on itself and others and is acted on by them. Consequently, even the universal individual called "God" must be conceived as having two essential aspects: a relatively more active aspect in which it acts on or makes a difference to both itself and all others and a relatively more passive aspect in which all others as well as itself act on or make a difference to it. Thus the uniqueness of God in comparison with all other individuals does not lie, as classical Christian theology has held, in God's only acting on others and in no way being acted on by them, but rather in the completely universal scope of God's field of interaction with others as well as with Godself. Whereas any other individual interacts with itself for a finite time only, God's acting on Godself and being acted on by Godself has never begun nor will it ever end. And so, too, with respect to interaction with others: whereas any individual other than God interacts with some others only, God interacts with all, not only acting on them but also being acted on by them.

In both aspects, God as the universal individual is strictly unsurpassable; and only by being thus unsurpassable both actively and passively can God be the God necessarily implied by the distinctive double structure of Christian faith, and thus be both the ground of unreserved trust and the object of unqualified loyalty. We may trust in God without reservation only because God is unsurpassably active, ever doing all that could conceivably be done by anyone for all others as well as Godself. Likewise, we may be loyal to God without qualification only because God is unsurpassably passive, being ever open to all that could conceivably be done or suffered by anyone as something that is also done to God.

It is for the best of reasons, then, that Christian theology has traditionally understood God to be both all-good and all-powerful. To be both unsurpassably active and unsurpassably passive in one's interaction with others is to be precisely unsurpassably good and unsurpassably powerful, since goodness and power alike have both active and passive aspects as applied to individuals. An individual's goodness toward others is always, first of all, openness to their interests and only then action furthering their interests on the basis of such openness. Similarly, an individual's power in relation to others is never merely the capacity to act on them, but is also always the capacity to be acted on by them. The great tragedy of traditional theology, of course, is that this has been forgotten in thinking and speaking about God, whose goodness and power have been classically conceived one-sidedly as wholly active. Thus God's power has been understood as "omnipotence," in the sense of all the power there is, as distinct from all the power that any one individual could have consistently with there being other individuals also having power, however minimal. The result is that classical Christian theology has been saddled with an insoluble problem of evil. If God's is a sheer monopoly of power, then it cannot be true both that God is also omnibeneficent or all-good and that evil of some kind or in some form is real or exists.

Once allow, however, that God's is not the only power, and the problem of evil is capable of solution. Such evil as is real or exists can then be accounted for by the decision or agency of other powers, and God can without difficulty be said to be all-good as well as all-powerful. This is so, at any rate, if allowing that there are powers other than God need not deny that God is unsurpassably powerful as well as unsurpassably good.

But now what does all this have to do with the inappropriateness of Christian exclusivism? The connection, I maintain, is this: by establishing, in effect, a double standard for obtaining salvation, exclusivism creates a form of the problem of evil to which there can be no such solution. I say that exclusivism establishes a double standard, because, as I have shown, it implies that the human predicament of the vast majority of men and women is radically different from that of the tiny minority who have been able to become Christians by being encountered by the Christian proclamation. Through no fault of their own, by far most human beings have been allowed to remain in their sin without any prospect of salvation. But this, clearly, is an evil; in fact, on exclusivism's own presuppositions, it must be an evil of the first magnitude that all but a few persons are left utterly without hope and are finally lost. It is also an evil, however, that logically compels one to deny either that God is all-powerful or that God is all-good. For in the nature of the case, it is not an evil that can be accounted for by any decision or agency other than God's own. In the case of other forms of evil—such as, for example, the evil of sin or the moral evil committed by human beings or by other beings created with moral freedom—such a "free will defense" of the all-goodness and the all-powerfulness of God is at least available. But in this case, there is no possibility of arguing in this way; for, as we have seen, the fact, if it were a fact, that by far most human beings, having once forfeited their possibility of existing in faith, would then have no prospect of ever actualizing it would be due, not to their own decision or agency, but to God's— specifically to God's abandoning them to their predicament instead of so acting as to liberate them from it, as God would have done for at least the few human beings who are in a position to become Christians.

I conclude, therefore, that there is no escaping the problem of evil that is necessarily implied by exclusivism. If exclusivism were true, the only inference from the fact that by far most human beings could have no hope of salvation would be either that God is not good enough to want them to be saved or that God is not powerful enough to do all that anyone could do to save them, except what they must do themselves. Either way, the understanding of God necessarily implied by Christian faith, as at once unsurpassably good and unsurpassably powerful, could no longer be upheld.

Recognizing this, we may confirm my judgment that exclusivism is deeply inappropriate to Jesus Christ and that, for this reason, also, the case against it is unusually strong. We may also insist over against it that, if the Christian understanding of God as unsurpassable in both goodness and power is really to be maintained, no woman or man can ever be without the possibility of existing in faith as soon and as long as she or he is a human being at all.

CHAPTER 3

Difficulties with the Case for Pluralism

The burden of the last chapter was to show that the case against exclusivism is exceptionally strong—and that this is true not only because exclusivism is an incredible theological position, being incapable of validation in terms of common human experience and reason, but also because it is deeply inappropriate to Jesus Christ. Implying, as it does, a double standard for obtaining salvation, exclusivism creates a form of the problem of evil that is insoluble. If it were true, the only inference from the fact that Christians alone are saved would be either that God is not good enough to want to save all others or that God is not powerful enough to make their salvation possible. Either way, the understanding of God implied by the assertion that Jesus is the Christ could not be consistently upheld.

If this argument is sound, we have good reason to look to some option other than exclusivism for the answer to our central question. It is by no means obvious, however, that it is to pluralism that we should look. We have seen, to be sure, that pluralists are wont to claim over against inclusivists that their position is the only consistent alternative to exclusivism. But there are difficulties with their argument for pluralism, not the least of which is why this claim itself should be thought valid (cf. Ogden 1988).

To see why I say this, we need to recall just what it is that Christians and theologians who contend for pluralism understand by it. I argued at the end of Chapter 1 that, contrary to what might be supposed from the recent statements of certain pluralists, the position they hold is not only that there *can be* many true religions, but that there actually *are*. Thus the assertion typical of pluralism is that Christianity is not the only true religion, but, in John Hick's words, "one of a plurality of contexts of salvation . . . within which the transformation of human existence from self-centeredness to God- or Reality-centeredness is occurring." Such an assertion, Hick claims, is the "logical" (or "natural") conclusion of the trajectory whose path can be traced "from an exclusivist to an inclusivist view of other religions" (Hick and Knitter, 23, 16, 22). But how valid is this claim?

In the earlier discussion of exclusivism and inclusivism as both forms of religious monism, I noted that the reason for their claim that Christianity alone *is* the true religion is the, for them, very good reason that it alone *can be* formally true. Because in their views the only religion that can be true in this sense is the religion established by God in the unique saving event of Jesus Christ, they can confidently assert that the Christian religion alone is true in this sense because there simply cannot be many ways of salvation of which the Christian way is only one. But, then, this is the assertion, common to both monistic views, that has to be countered if there is to be a complete break with monism, whether exclusivistic or inclusivistic. To counter it, however, in no way requires one to assert with pluralism that there actually *are* many ways of salvation of which Christianity is but one. All that one needs to assert is that there *can be* these many ways, even if, as a matter of fact, Christianity should turn out to be the only way of salvation there is.

For this reason, Hick's claim is unfounded. Pluralism is not the logical conclusion of a consistent movement away from exclusivism, but is an independent assertion to be evaluated on its merits. Exclusivism and inclusivism could both be invalidated without in any way validating pluralism as the answer to our question.

Unfortunately, this is not the only logical difficulty with the typical case for pluralism. Among other fallacious arguments that pluralists sometimes offer is that genuine interreligious dialogue is possible only on the basis of a consistent pluralism. Thus Alan Race, for instance, commends "pluralism in the Christian theology of religions" because it "seeks to draw the faiths of the world's religious past into a mutual recognition of one another's truths and values, in order for truth itself to come into proper focus" (Race, 148). But no such mutual recognition of one another's truths and values is logically required in order for truth itself to come into proper focus. All that is necessary to this end is a mutual recognition of one another's truth- and value-*claims* as exactly that—*claims* to validity that are equally in need and equally deserving of critical validation in terms of our common human experience and reason. Implied by such recognition, no doubt, is the further recognition of one another as persons, who can make and validate such claims and who are, therefore, entitled to a distinctive kind of moral respect. But such mutual respect for one another as persons in no way depends upon asserting that the claims to truth and value of either person are valid claims. I can be wrong, and so can my partner; and yet both of us can and should be open to one another in genuine dialogue and in a common inquiry into the true and the good.

In short, the case for pluralism can no more be made by arguing *for* interreligious dialogue than by arguing *against* religious monism; and to reason in either way on the contrary supposition is to reason fallaciously. Pluralism is not the logical conclusion of a consistent movement toward the other religions, but is an independent assertion that must stand or fall on its own. Interreligious dialogue could very well be validated without in the least validating pluralism as the answer to our question (cf. Lochhead).

Nor can validating it ever be easy by the very logic of such an answer. Whether any religion at all is true must, in the nature of the case, be more or less difficult to determine. We noted one of the principal reasons for this already in the first chapter, when we considered the procedures necessary to determine religious truth. Because these procedures require verifying the necessary implications of a religion for both belief and action, they unavoidably involve all the well-known difficulties of both metaphysical and ethical verification. For this reason alone, one might well hesitate to pronounce any religion true, much less a plurality of them.

But not only are there such philosophical difficulties; there are historical and hermeneutical difficulties as well. Every religion is a historical emergent, and it is available concretely, as just this or that specific religion, only in and through the religious praxis of some particular social and cultural group. Furthermore, every religious tradition is to some extent self-defining in that it specifies certain of its elements as normative for some or all of the others. But these normative elements, no less than all the rest, are thoroughly historical and are accessible as such only empirically, through historical experience and inquiry. Thus what counts as formally normative for a particular religion both in principle and in fact must be determined historically by actually encountering its particular tradition. And such determination may very well be complicated by the fact that there is no consensus in the religion about what is normative for its tradition. Indeed, its tradition so-called may turn out to be little more than a plurality of religious traditions, each specifying what is normative for it in a somewhat different way.

Yet even after one determines what is to count as normative for a religion, there remain the by no means minor difficulties of rightly interpreting its norms so that they can perform their proper function. No norm can function as such except by being somehow understood; and yet how it is to be rightly understood is likely to be even more controversial than whether it or something else is really normative. This would be true, in fact, even if there were agreement, as there is not, that religious claims are properly analyzed as existential claims and as therefore having an existential kind of meaning and truth. Exactly what it means to say this, and thus how religious claims are and are not related to other logically distinct kinds of claims, continue to be matters of controversy among philosophers and students of religion as well as theologians. In any event, whether what this or that specific religion offers as its answer to the existential question is true cannot be determined merely philosophically. As also in part a properly historical and hermeneutical question, it can be answered only by actually encountering the specific religion and rightly interpreting what it asserts or implies about the meaning of ultimate reality for us.

Naturally, to be a religious believer is one and the same with claiming either explicitly or implicitly that one's own religion is true. But, aside from the fact that this is simply one more claim to religious truth, whose validity also has to be determined along with that of every other, all that its being validated would allow one to affirm a priori about the truth of any other specific religion is that it either can or cannot be true. Thus, even assuming that, from a Christian standpoint, not only exclusivism but inclusivism also could be shown to be invalid, the most that a Christian could possibly know, prior to actually encountering the many religions and rightly interpreting them, is not that they in fact are true, but only that they at least can be true.

Of course, it is not particularly difficult to undertake the empirical study of religion, or of specific religions, and to do this, as we say, comparatively. In this way, one can learn, for example, that human beings quite generally, after a certain amount of social and cultural development, seem to feel the need for some sort of radical transformation of their own individual existence in relation to ultimate reality. Thus not only Christianity but all of the other axial religions as well are evidently addressed to this need and present themselves as the means of just such ultimate transformation. But learning only this about the axial religions entitles one to make no more than a purely formal statement about them—to the effect that they all exhibit the same essential structure both in focusing the existential problem in the individual person and in seeking to solve it by radically transforming her or his self-understanding. Such a statement in no way excludes, but obviously allows for, a wide range of material differences, not excluding substantial contrariety and contradiction, between one religion and another in their respective understandings of human existence.

The great difficulty for pluralists, however, is to get beyond this purely formal statement in a reasoned way. If there are many true religions, the similarities between them, notwithstanding all their differences, must be material as well as formal, matters of content as well as of structure. In other words, with whatever differences in concepts and symbols, they must express substantially the same self-understanding, the same way of understanding ourselves in relation to others and the whole. And this means, for reasons explained in the first chapter, that they must also have substantially the same necessary implications, both metaphysical and ethical. But if my own experience of inter-religious dialogue is any indication, it is likely to remain exceedingly difficult, even after the most extensive study and first-hand experience of another person's religious claims, to know just where, or even whether, one's own religion expresses the same religious truth.

This has come home to me with particular force during the course of my involvement in Buddhist-Christian dialogue. For over a decade now, I have been engaged, in one way or another, in extended discussion with Buddhists, especially with certain members of the Kyoto School of Japanese Zen Buddhism. As this discussion has deepened, I have become increasingly convinced that, for all of the obvious differences between the formulations of our respective positions, there are striking similarities between the understanding of human existence for which my Zen Buddhist partners typically argue and what I as a Christian theologian understand to be our authentic self-understanding as human beings. I realize, of course, that my understanding of authentic existence is not the only Christian understanding of faith in God, any more than their understanding of authenticity is the only Buddhist understanding of the realization of emptiness. But fully recognizing that the discussion between us is only part of the larger Buddhist-Christian dialogue, I am still struck by the convergence between their self-understanding as Buddhists and my own as a Christian. In fact, when I apply my existentialist equivalent of a pragmatist criterion of meaning—according to which different formulations that make no difference in how one must understand oneself to appropriate them are insofar only verbally different—I strongly incline to think that such real differences as there may be between our two self-understandings can only be rather subtle and hard to pin down.

Thus I am quite unable to share the view often expressed by other Christians and theologians that, despite their obvious formal similarity as axial religions, or religions of ultimate transformation, Buddhism and Christianity are deeply opposed understandings of human existence. Contrary to the claim that, for Buddhism, the human problem is focused on our sheer existence as fragmentary beings, I find that Buddhist talk of the deepest level of human suffering identifies it as an ignorance of our essential condition which is not merely a matter of fate, but for which we are each in some way responsible. To this extent, there is a clear parallel, if not a convergence, between the Buddhist understanding of suffering as the consequence of ignorance and the Christian understanding of death as the wages of sin. This is clear, at any rate, if we avoid not only a naturalistic misunderstanding of what Buddhists mean by ignorance but also a moralistic misunderstanding of what Christians mean by sin. Provided sin is understood, as it should be, not as moral transgression, but as the deeper refusal of one's existence as a creature of God, it is not merely one among the many options of our freedom, but our "natural" condition, the basic state of existence, or way of understanding ourselves, in which we ordinarily exist. Thus, in the Christian understanding, existence in sin and death is, in its way, a matter of destiny as well as of freedom, even as, in the Buddhist view, existence in ignorance and suffering is, in its way, a matter of freedom as well as of destiny.

Likewise, I do not find that the Buddhist understanding of authentic existence is the kind of ahistorical and world-denying understanding that it is commonly taken to be. On the contrary, I see my Buddhist colleagues being at least as concerned as Christians are with the whole range of human needs, of body and mind as well as of soul and spirit, and hence as turned toward the world and history, not away from them. Nor am I able to explain this simply by their being modern women and men who have been shaped as much as modern Christians have by historical consciousness and by the resultant sense of responsibility to transform the entire setting of human life, social and cultural as well as natural. As much as they have indeed been influenced by modern secularity, they have the confidence, which I take to be entirely justified, that the deepest roots of their commitment to transforming social and cultural structures as well as individual persons lie in their own religious tradition as Buddhists. Just as for Christians any living faith cannot fail to be active in love, so for Buddhists the wisdom that overcomes our ignorance must inevitably express itself in compassion. Given a modern sense of historical responsibility, then, compassion, like love, must concern itself not only with meeting human needs within societies and cultures, but also with transforming their basic structures so as to overcome injustice and oppression (see Habito; Ray).

Consequently, when my Buddhist colleagues talk of what it means to exist authentically, they seem to point to something like the same genuinely dialectical, or "paradoxical," way of existing to which I seek to point as a Christian. On the one hand, it is an existence in radical freedom *from* oneself and the world, in which one is inwardly released from clinging to them in ignorance and suffering or in sin and death; on the other hand, it is an existence in radical freedom *for* oneself and the world, in which one is inwardly released to affirm and to further them in compassion or in love (see Park).

True as all this is, however, I still have not been able to conclude that Buddhism and Christianity are really only different formulations of the same understanding of existence. Subtle as their real differences may be, there nonetheless seem to me to be such; and up to now, at least, I have not found any way of reducing them. This becomes particularly clear whenever I consider not only Buddhist and Christian self-understandings as such, but also their metaphysical implications.

Of course, one has to be careful at this point to distinguish clearly between the metaphysical implications of a given self-understanding and the metaphysical consequences of some particular formulation of it. Just as a self-understanding is one thing, its explicit formulation in particular concepts and symbols, something else, so the necessary implications of a self-understanding ought never to be confused with the consequences that follow, given certain concepts and symbols in which it happens to be formulated. This means, among other things, that one must always allow for the possibility that what are widely supposed to be the metaphysical implications of a self-understanding are not really that at all, but are simply the metaphysical consequences of a particular way of formulating it, or of the assumptions made in doing so. Thus, for example, it is at least arguable that the traditional Christian doctrine of the impassibility of God follows, not from a Christian self-understanding as such, but rather from certain metaphysical assumptions about who God has to be that were made more or less uncritically by the church fathers who classically formulated it. But even if one allows that something like this may also be the case in Buddhism, the fact remains that what are widely supposed to be the metaphysical implications of Buddhist self-understanding are really and significantly different from what I, for one, take to be necessarily implied by a Christian understanding of existence.

This is clear enough from the differences indicated by Christian theism, on the one hand, and Buddhist nontheism, on the other. Whereas for Christians, the self-understanding of faith necessarily implies the reality of God as the sole primal source and the sole final end of all things, for

Buddhists, the self-understanding of wisdom is held to imply, rather, the dependent coorigination of all things and their essential emptiness. So, according to Christianity, the world and history develop irreversibly from the past into the future, and the relations between things are external as well as internal, grounding real differences between them. According to Buddhism, on the contrary, nothing whatever is or can be independent and self-existing, because everything is of necessity interdependent with, and interpenetrated by, everything else. But if this is the ultimate metaphysical truth about things, then any development from the past into the future is reversible, and either there are no relations between things at all or else all relations between them are internal only, and any differences between things sufficient to ground differential thought and action with respect to them are ultimately delusive.

With this, however, the rationale for responsible thought and action in and for the world clearly seems to be undercut. For if it need not imply that we are to be concerned for nothing at all, it does imply something hardly less stultifying of responsible thought and action—namely, that we are to be equally concerned for everything. Thus there at least appears to be a basic contradiction between the kind of metaphysical monism that Buddhist self-understanding is widely supposed to imply and this self-understanding as such, especially the development of it by contemporary Buddhists who are clearly as concerned as modern Christians are with responsibly making history and transforming the world (cf. Ogden 1990).

Whether or not such a contradiction is real, or how it is to be resolved, is not my present concern. I have gone into it only to explain why, on the basis of my own continuing encounter with Buddhism, I am still not able to say that its understanding of existence is materially the same as Christianity's. For all of their striking similarities, they still seem to me to be really different, at least as they have been formulated up to now. Therefore, I have more and more found myself agreeing with the observation of Clifford Geertz that "what all sacred symbols assert is that the good for man is to live realistically; where they differ is in the vision of reality they construct" (Geertz, 130). Clearly, a serious difficulty in making any case for pluralism is coming to terms with this difference.

There are still other difficulties, however, pertaining to the evidence and argument that at least some pluralists offer to support their claim that there are many true religions or ways of salvation. Thus John Hick, notably, assumes that the evidence appropriate to validating the claim is provided by "the fruits of religious faith in human life," and so by the extent of individual and social transformation effected by the different specific religions (Hick and Knitter, 23–24). As a matter of fact, Hick appears to feel confirmed in his pluralistic position primarily on the negative ground that none of the axial religions, taken as a whole, proves to be superior to the others when they are all assessed in terms of their effectiveness as contexts of salvation or liberation, both individual and social (Hick 1989, 297–380). But this way of arguing for the equality, or "rough parity," of the axial religions, and hence for pluralism, will not stand up under close scrutiny.

This is clear, first of all, from the fact that there is no valid inference from the so-called fruits of religious faith in human life to the reality or presence of such faith itself. It is indeed the case, for reasons explained in the first chapter, that any religious faith as an understanding of human existence has necessary implications for ethical action as well as for metaphysical belief. And its ethical implications may very well extend to transforming the structures of society and culture as well as to the transformation of individual moral behavior. But to do what faith would do, or to act as faith would act, is not necessarily to exist in faith itself, any more than believing what faith would believe is possible only for a person of faith. And this is true even if we prescind altogether from the case of insincere or hypocritical action. Even if one does what faith would do, or acts as it would act, in all sincerity, one may or may not understand oneself in faith and act on the basis of it instead of something else. Thus, in the well-known passage from his correspondence with the Corinthians, Paul can say of even the apparently most radical expressions of love that one can give away all that one has and even sacrifice one's life, and yet "have not love" (1 Cor 13:3).

I realize, naturally, that what Paul and other Christians can say about the radical transformation of faith working through love applies, in the first instance, to Christian faith, rather than to religious faith more generally. But I have the distinct impression that much the same thing could be said about the radical transformation to which any of the other axial religions points in its own understanding of human existence. Although any such transformation must indeed bear fruits both in individual moral behavior and in the structures of society and culture, it itself takes place solely in our innermost self-understanding, and, therefore, can never be either simply identified with its fruits or validly inferred from them, however validly they can be inferred from it.

There is another closely related objection to this whole way of reasoning. Granted that individual and social changes can indeed be observed to occur in the context of a specific religion, how does one rule out the possibility that changes thus associated with the religion have nonetheless occurred independently of it or been effected less because of it than in spite of it? One of the striking things to me about the behavior of human beings in extreme situations is that their specific religious or philosophical affiliations seem to make relatively little difference. During the Nazi time in Germany, for instance, the resistance against Hitler included persons of the most diverse religious and philosophical persuasions, even as the same was true of those who passively supported his regime or actively collaborated with it. I submit that the case is not likely to be different in other more or less similar situations familiar to all of us. But, then, what force can there be in arguing for the truth of a specific religion from changes occurring in either individuals or societies in its particular context?

The still deeper difficulty, however, is with the underlying assumption of any such argument—namely, that the truth of a specific religion could be logically determined from its effectiveness as a context of salvation or liberation. To make this assumption is to fall into a serious logical confusion—as serious, indeed, as if we were to suppose that the truth of ordinary judgments of fact could be determined from their effectiveness in getting themselves sincerely believed. To believe ever so sincerely that a factual judgment is true is to do nothing whatever from which its truth could be determined. If it is true, it is not because it is believed, but because it is worthy of belief, even if no one ever believed it; and whether this can or cannot be said depends entirely upon whether or not it can be validated by the procedures appropriate to verifying judgments of fact. In the same way, one may most sincerely understand oneself as a specific religion calls one to do without providing even the least reason for thinking that the religion is true. If it is true, it is not because one so understands oneself, but because one ought so to understand oneself, even if one were to fail to do so; and whether this is or is not the case entirely depends upon whether or not one's self-understanding can be validated by the procedures appropriate to determining religious truth. For this reason, the extent to which a specific religion is effective in securing even the most committed adherents is logically irrelevant to validating its claim to be formally true.

Yet even if pluralists were to take account of this and were to support their claim only by evidence and argument appropriate to doing so, they would still face a fundamental difficulty in making their case. This is so, at any rate, on the assumption that pluralism is indeed to be distinguished from complete relativism, by which I mean the position according to which all religions are formally true. According to Alan Race, "the pertinent question mark which hovers over all theories of pluralism is how far they succeed in overcoming the sense of 'debilitating relativism' which is their apparent danger." Thus Race explicitly rejects "the view that all faiths are equally true, or of equal value, or are ultimately saying the same thing," and insists that pluralists, in their way, in the way of genuine interreligious dialogue, must participate "in the search to distinguish the more from the less profound, the more from the less 'true' religious belief" (Race, 90, 143f.). In his clear intention to avoid complete relativism, Race seems to me to be representative of most of his fellow pluralists, even if, as I noted in an earlier chapter, a few of them have claimed, perhaps carelessly, that all religions are equally true or adequate. In any event, what I take pluralism to mean is significantly different from relativism in allowing that there at least can be specific religions, or ways of salvation, that are false rather than true.

But if pluralism does indeed allow this, there is no way of making a reasoned case for its claim that there are many true religions except by employing, either tacitly or openly, some norm of religious truth. If at least some specific religion can be false, no specific religion can be judged to be true without

'condition of the possibility'), that which unites the religions in common discourse and praxis, is *not* how they are related to the church, . . . or how they are related to Christ, . . . nor even how they respond to and conceive of God, but rather, to what extent they are promoting *Soteria* (in Christian images, the *basileia*)—to what extent they are engaged in promoting human welfare and bringing about liberation with and for the poor and nonpersons" (Hick and Knitter, 187).

Here, again, it seems to me that many of the intentions of pluralists are sound and that they have a contribution to make to our common theological task. In fact, I am particularly appreciative of Knitter's efforts because, in a rather different way from Hick's, they can help to develop a more adequate conceptuality in which to think and speak about religion and religions in a purely formal sense. The problem with the kind of existentialist conceptuality that I have developed and employed in these chapters is that it may be thought to isolate all that is properly religious from the specifically political aspect of praxis and culture with which Knitter and other liberation theologians are rightly concerned. By interpreting religion as explicit self-understanding at the level of primary culture, it allows well enough for the metaphysical and ethical implications of religion, but without making clear that its ethical implications always have a specifically political aspect. One value of Knitter's expressly, although not exclusively, political understanding of "*soteria*" is that it can help to clarify this, so that one can say, as I have stressed elsewhere, that the existentialist interpretation of religion must always be also its political interpretation (see Ogden 1982, 89–96, 148–68; 1986, 143–50).

But the point of Knitter's soteriocentrism is clearly more than any such purely formal point. Anomalous as it may seem for a pluralist to do so, he undoubtedly formulates the norm by which he proposes to judge the truth of all specific religions. If pluralism in his view is valid, it is because there is not only one religion that satisfies this norm, but many—many religions that are more or less equally engaged in promoting human welfare and liberating the poor and oppressed. As a matter of fact, Knitter goes so far as to make this norm "the basis and goal for interreligious dialogue" and the "condition of the possibility" of "mutual understanding and cooperation between the religions." But this only shows the more clearly that in this respect, at least, the difference between his soteriocentric pluralism and the inclusivism that he rejects is not a difference in principle but only a difference in fact. Whereas inclusivists appeal to the salvation constituted by the event of Jesus Christ, Knitter appeals to the salvation to be realized by following the historical Jesus in his service of God's kingdom, and thus in promoting liberation and transforming the world (Knitter 1988, 33–48). In both cases, however, the norms appealed to are provided by some one specific religion or philosophy, which is thereby made normative for all the others.

There is, to be sure, this significant difference between Knitter's Christian pluralism and Christian inclusivism: whereas for inclusivism there not only is but can be only one religion that is formally true, for pluralism there not only can be but are many religions that are true in this sense. Thus Knitter is express in saying that it is "for Christians" that the norm of religious truth is as he formulates it, leaving open the possibility, which inclusivism precludes, that persons of other faiths express substantially the same truth even while validly formulating different formal norms for judging it. But important as this difference certainly is, it in no way alters the fact that Knitter employs a norm of judgment as surely as inclusivists do and that his norm, like theirs, is derived from some one religion or philosophy, as distinct from any of the others that may express substantially the same religious truth.

The moral of this whole development seems obvious. Claims of pluralists to the contrary notwithstanding, pluralism in no way offers an alternative to employing some norm of religious truth, and thus to making some one religion or philosophy normative for judging all the rest. Provided that pluralism is distinct from complete relativism, there is simply no other way to make good its claim that more than one specific religion is formally true. The relevant question, then, is not *whether* a norm is to be employed, but only *how*: openly and critically, with the clear recognition that even one's norm may be problematic and need to be validated; or, rather, tacitly and uncritically, without allowing for the possibility that validating one's norm itself may also be required. And here, ironically enough, a pluralist like Knitter can speak of his norm as itself the "basis and goal for interreligious dialogue," while an inclusivist such as Gavin D'Costa can allow that the "possibility and risk" of abandoning his Christian beliefs and even being converted "cannot be discounted if dialogue is genuinely open and trusting" (D'Costa, 121).

At any rate, it should now be clear that there are a number of difficulties with the case for pluralism and that they are sufficiently serious to make it doubtful whether it can be a valid answer to our question. Like exclusivism, it is logically an extreme position. This is evident from the fact that it counters exclusivism's claim that there cannot be more than one religion that is formally true, not with the contradictory claim that there can be, but with the contrary claim that there is, that there are many religions that are true in this sense of the word. The difficulty with extreme contraries on any issue, however, is that, while both cannot be true, both can be false. Therefore, it is entirely possible that pluralism's claim that there are many true religions is as false as the claim of exclusivism that cannot be more than one, which, as we have seen, is the real meaning of its contrary answer to our question.

If the argument of this chapter is sound, one may well ask whether this is not, in fact, the case. But, then, one must look beyond pluralism as well as exclusivism for the answer to our question, as I propose to do in the concluding chapter.

CHAPTER 4

Beyond the Usual Options

In preceding chapters, I considered two of the three main ways in which our central question is usually answered—namely, exclusivism and pluralism. So far as exclusivism is concerned, the results of this consideration were strongly negative, since it proved to be not only incapable of validation as credible in terms of common human experience and reason, but also deeply inappropriate to Jesus Christ. In the case of pluralism, the results of my consideration were skeptical rather than negative. I argued that there are a number of difficulties with the case that pluralists make for it and that these difficulties are sufficiently serious to make one question its validity. Certainly unfounded, I held, is the claim that pluralism is the only consistent alternative to exclusivism. In point of fact, the position that there are many true religions is logically as extreme as the contrary position of exclusivism that there can be only one; and so invalidating exclusivism, and inclusivism as well, would in no way validate pluralism, since both positions, being contraries, could very well be false, even though both could not be true. Still other difficulties pertaining to the evidence and argument that pluralists offer and, above all, to establishing more than merely formal similarities between different religions raise doubts whether they have yet succeeded in making their case.

Assuming now that these results are sound, we might be tempted to conclude, in the light of our analysis of the usual options, that it is to the third option of inclusivism that we should look for a valid answer to our question. After all, it is significantly different from both of the other positions; and considering what I have said about the common difficulty of logical contraries, we might expect it to provide something like a mean between the two extremes.

We would be encouraged in this, naturally, by inclusivists, who tend to think of themselves as occupying just such a third, mediating position between the other more extreme positions. But there is a problem in agreeing with them about this, as should be clear from what has already been said— namely, that inclusivism in its way is also an extreme position. Significantly different as it is from exclusivism in asserting that a decision for Christ's salvation is in some way a universal possibility for each and every human being, it is nonetheless essentially similar to exclusivism in its monistic insistence that Christianity alone is the formally true religion. Like exclusivists, inclusivists hold that the only religion that even can be true in this sense is the religion established by God in the unique saving event of Jesus Christ. Therefore, even though they allow that non-Christians can be saved by Christ anonymously and unknowingly outside of the visible church and that any religion transformed by his salvation can itself be substantially true and a means of salvation, they still maintain that his is the only salvation and that it is mediated explicitly and knowingly as such solely by the Christian religion. To this extent, inclusivists are no less extreme than exclusivists or pluralists in their answer to our question.

Here, again, of course, I am speaking in terms of an ideal type of theological position, not of the positions actually held by this or that theologian or group of theologians. What I mean by inclusivists are simply those who hold the theological position that I have just defined, however they may otherwise be identified or identify themselves. Essential to the inclusivistic position thus understood, however, is the same logically extreme claim essential to exclusivism, to the effect that there not only is but can be only one true religion, in the sense that Christianity alone can validly claim to be formally true.

Recognizing this, we may well hesitate to conclude that inclusivism is the option we are seeking. And such hesitation will seem the more prudent if we reflect that in the case of many a disputed question the usual options for answering it are not the only answers that are logically possible. On the contrary, nothing is more common than disputes that stubbornly persist precisely because the disputants insist upon both themselves choosing and forcing others to choose between only some of the possible options, any one of which is about as good or as bad as the others.

That something like this may be true of the question before us in these chapters appears to me extremely likely. The several parties to the current discussion more and more tend to assume that the only ways open for answering it are the usual options of exclusivism, inclusivism, and pluralism. Even so, there is at least one other way of answering it that is a distinct alternative to all three of these usual ways, although it has not been clearly recognized, much less carefully considered, in the discussion up to now. It will be apparent, I am sure, that it is this fourth way that I judge to be the relatively more adequate option open to us. But whether or not I am right in this judgment, we can hardly expect to be clear about the issue raised for theology by the challenge of pluralism unless we at least take account of all of the main possibilities for answering our question. The purpose of what follows, then, even as of the preceding chapters, is not to settle this issue, by finally arguing for *the* answer to the question, but, rather, to clarify the issue itself, by at last attending to this neglected possibility for answering the question beyond the usual options.

I begin with a summary characterization of the fourth option in relation to the other three. At one extreme, we have religious, or, more exactly, Christian, monism in its two forms of exclusivism and inclusivism respectively. Common to both monistic positions is the claim that there not only is but can be only one true religion because Christianity alone can validly claim to be formally true. At the other extreme is religious, or Christian, pluralism, with its logically contrary position that there not only can be but are other religions whose claim to be formally true is as valid as Christianity's. Now, as I showed in the last chapter, there is no need to assert Christian pluralism in order to make a complete break with Christian monism, whether exclusivistic or inclusivistic. What one needs to assert to counter monism is not that there actually *are* many true religions, but only that there *can be,* this being the logical contradictory of any position that there *cannot be* because Christianity alone can be true. But if this assertion is clearly as distinct from pluralism as it is contradictory of monism, it could also be true even if the assertion of pluralism were false or the case for it still had to be made. One could hold, in other words, that religions other than Christianity can also be formally true even if, in point of fact, none of them actually is true or has as yet been shown to be so in a reasoned way.

This is the position that I take to be the fourth option open to Christians and theologians for answering our central question. What I want to do in the remainder of the chapter is to explain what is and is not involved in holding it, at least in the form in which I should wish to do so. In doing this, I shall be further elaborating its differences from the other options, especially inclusivism, whose claims to validity remain to be considered.

The essential difference between the two monistic options, on the one hand, and the fourth option, on the other, is that they deny what it affirms— namely, that religions other than Christianity can as validly claim to be formally true as it can. If we ask now what underlies and explains this essential difference, the answer can only be a difference in christology. By this I mean that, while in each case there is a way of thinking and speaking about Jesus as of decisive significance for human existence, there is nonetheless a difference between these two ways amounting to a difference in christological type. One way of trying to formulate this difference is to distinguish between a "christocentric" and a "theocentric" type of christology. But an obvious objection to this formulation is that both types of christology are, in their ways, christocentric as well as theocentric. Both understand Christian faith to be nothing other or less than faith in the one true God in whom alone is salvation, even as they both affirm that the only true God is the God who has in fact acted to save explicitly and decisively through Jesus Christ. Nevertheless, there is a crucial difference between their respective understandings of the unique saving event of Jesus Christ, which I prefer to formulate as follows: whereas for Christian monists, whether exclusivists or inclusivists, this event not only represents the possibility of salvation but also in some way *constitutes* it, for those holding the fourth position, this event in no way constitutes the possibility of salvation but only *represents* it.

I trust that the distinction I have employed here between a constitutive and a representative event is already familiar, in substance if not also under these particular labels. But if an ordinary example of it is needed, I know of none better than that provided by the old story about the conversation between the three baseball umpires. The youngest and least experienced umpire allows, "I call 'em as I see 'em." Whereupon the second umpire, being older and more sure of himself, claims, "I call 'em as they are." But to all this the oldest and shrewdest umpire responds with complete self-confidence, "They ain't nothin' till I call 'em!" By an event constitutive of the possibility of salvation I mean an event that is like the third umpire's calls in that the possibility of salvation is nothing until the event occurs. On the contrary, what I mean by an event representative of the possibility of salvation is an event similar to the calls of the second umpire in that it serves to declare a possibility of salvation that already is as it is prior to the event's occurring to declare it.

Another example of a representative event drawn from the explicitly religious context is a minister's solemnizing the marriage of a man and a woman. Since it is generally understood that a marriage is constituted as such by the man and woman themselves, each pledging troth to the other, the office of the minister is properly to represent or declare their union, in no way to constitute it. This is evident from the formula customarily used by the minister in performing the service: "Forasmuch as so and so have consented together in holy wedlock, . . . I pronounce that they are husband and wife together."

To be sure, other acts performed by Christian ministers are commonly thought to have a constitutive, rather than a merely representative, significance even with respect to salvation. This is particularly true of preaching the word and administering the sacraments, where they themselves are understood, as they typically are by exclusivists, to be constitutive of the possibility of salvation. Baptizing a person, for instance, may be viewed as itself effecting her or his transition from a state of sin to a state of grace, so that she or he could be expected to affirm, in the words of a well-known catechism, that baptism was the event "wherein I was made a member of Christ, the child of God, and an inheritor of the kingdom of heaven." But even for Christian inclusivists, any such view of baptism, or of any other means of salvation, is mistaken. Even in their understanding, all acts of the church's ministry and, for that matter, even the church itself are representative of the possibility of salvation rather than constitutive of it—whence their rejection of the claim of exclusivists that there is no salvation outside of the church.

An alternative view of baptism that I have long found instructive was resourcefully defended already in the nineteenth century by the Anglican theologian, Frederick W. Robertson. Like others of his contemporaries, such as Frederick Denison Maurice and Charles Kingsley, Robertson particularly struggled to understand the language of the Anglican Catechism to which I just alluded and according to which one is "made" a child of God in baptism. Believing, as he put it, that "baptism could not make me a child of God unless I were one by reason of my Humanity already," he sought to identify uses of the verb "to make" that were supportive of his belief. The results of his search are well represented by the teaching he prepared for his candidates for confirmation, in the questions and answers on baptism:

Q. What is baptism?

A. The authoritative declaration of a fact.

Q. What fact?

A. That I am God's child.

Q. Why then do you say that I am so *made,* in baptism?

A. Being *made,* I mean—*declared to be.*

Q. Explain what you mean.

A. As soon as a king dies, his successor is king. Coronation *declares the fact* but does not make him king. He was one before, but it corroborates, declares, affirms, seals the fact by a recognized form used for that purpose.

Elsewhere, Robertson uses the same illustration slightly differently, arguing that "a sovereign is made king by coronation, but only because he was *de jure* such before." And he confirms a similar sense of "to make" by means of a further illustration: "At mid-day, at sea, after the observation of the sun's altitude has been taken, the following form takes place: The commander asks, what is the hour? The reply is, 12 o'clock. He then rejoins, *make it so!* No act of his can literally determine mid-day; that is one of the facts of the universe, but that authoritative declaration in a most important sense does *make* it 12 o'clock, it makes it 12 o'clock *to them;* it regulates their hours, their views, the arrangement of their daily life, their whole course. . . . So does baptism—pronouncing the fact in God's name to exist, *make* that real on earth which, in itself real before, was unreal to those to whom the ratification had not been shown" (Brooke, 269, 513, 336, 513f.).

The most striking thing about Robertson's view is the analogy he clearly suggests between baptism thus understood and the Christ event itself. "The great fact for which the Redeemer died," he says, is "that all mankind are, *de jure,* God's sons, and that He bids them become such *de facto.*" If this kind of statement is evidently consistent with the traditional doctrine of the death of Christ as the "meritorious cause" of our salvation, Robertson's more characteristic way of making the same point is to say simply that the fact of our being God's children, which belongs to all humanity, "was revealed by Christ." "Christ revealed the fact that all men are God's children," and as the gospel which proclaims this is "the message to the *world,*" so "baptism is that message to the *individual.*" "Baptism is the grand special revelation to an individual by name, *A, B,* or *C,* of the great truth Christ revealed for the race, that all, Greeks and barbarians, are the children of God. It is the fact which they are to believe, a fact before they believe it, else how could they be asked to believe it?" (337, 336, 268). Robertson does not also say, to be sure, that this fact was true before Christ's revelation of it, and without his revelation. But this seems to be the clear implication of his analogy between baptism's revelation of the fact to the individual person and Christ's revelation of it to the world.

Of course, it is the whole point of analogy to allow for difference as well as similarity. And one might entirely agree with Robertson's view of baptism even while holding that the significance of the Christ event for salvation is different precisely in being somehow constitutive of its possibility rather than merely representative of it. This, in fact, is just the position typically taken by contemporary inclusivists, some of whom can be quite radical in their insistence on the strictly representative significance of all that is specifically Christian.

Thus Clodovis Boff, for instance, vigorously protests against the traditional identification of salvation, on the one hand, with revelation and faith, on the other. Just as in general there is "a distinction between the *real* and the *known*," so one must clearly distinguish between "salvation" and "consciousness or awareness of salvation (revelation, faith, church, sacraments, theology, and so on)." "Salvation touches every person, whereas revelation is specific to those alone to whom it has been *given* to become aware of this same salvation—to Christians." Accordingly, Boff proposes "a recasting of 'salvation history' as revelation history—as the history of the *revelation* of salvation. . . . 'Salvation history' would then be the history of salvation manifested, acknowledged, proclaimed—not the history of salvation as such." At the same time, revelation would be conceived as "a derived moment in the global history of humankind—a second moment, a moment 'with a lag.'" Far from reaching human beings universally, "it would perhaps pertain to its essence to be, and necessarily, a sectorial phenomenon only—charged, however, with a *metonymic* (*pars pro toto*), symbolic (*sacramentum salutis*) value" (Boff, 97, 99).

Boff realizes, naturally, that any such recasting raises "the towering question" of "the function of the economy of salvation." But this question can be answered, he believes, if, although only if, "it is possible to demonstrate that scripture, and the events reported there, as well as the whole salvific order of the church, are, where salvation is concerned, not of the order of its *constitution,* but of the order of its *manifestation."* In that event, "we would be dealing with a *hermeneutic* of salvation, not a *history* of salvation. Christianity would then be the *interpretation* of the salvation of the world, and not the salvation of the world itself, or even the exclusive instrument of this salvation" (97f.).

Having said this, however, Boff immediately blocks any inference that his is a representative type of christology. "More delicate," he says, "is the particular, and central, case of Jesus Christ, whom faith confesses as savior, and not merely as prophet, sage, or saint." True, "we must recognize that the church began very early to theologize the salvation brought by Jesus in less than totally intimate linkage to its proclamation (revelation) and explicit acceptance (faith)." Even in the New Testament there are "universalizing interpretations" that divorce salvation from revelation, and this position has remained "a constant in the history of Christian thought" from the church fathers right up to our own time. Recognizing this, "we are . . . led to admit of a salvation *antecedent and exterior to revelation* —antecedent to and outside the historical Jesus—not, however, independent of the *Kyrios* of glory" (98). But if all this seems rather to support a representative christology than to tell against it, there are clear indications elsewhere that this can hardly be Boff's intention. On the contrary, he speaks of "a *constitutive* reference of the human being to the person of Jesus Christ," and asserts that "the single real order of salvation" is "the christic order," which is "an ontic dimension, established in and for human beings, on the plane of their divine calling, and independent of their awareness." Thus "the Christian is precisely that human being in whom this constitutive reference emerges on the plane of consciousness. In the Christian, the ontic dimension is rendered onto-*logical*: the implicit reference becomes explicit, the latent reality becomes patent. . . . Thus the Christian is the *person who knows.* Christians know their reference to Jesus Christ, and know that all human beings have this same reference" (122).

For Boff, then, the event of Jesus Christ clearly is a special case, as compared with Christians and Christianity and all that is specifically Christian, whether faith and revelation or church and sacraments. Unlike the history of the church and all the rest of "salvation history," this event, at least, really is *history* of salvation, as distinct from its "revelation," its "hermeneutic," or its "interpretation." In the terms of Boff's own distinction, Jesus Christ is of the order of the *constitution* of salvation, not merely of the order of its *manifestation.*

This same position, as I have said, is typically taken by other Christian inclusivists, Protestant as well as Roman Catholic. Recognizing with Boff that Christian faith confesses Jesus Christ "as savior, and not merely as prophet, sage, or saint," they uphold a constitutive, rather than a representative, type of christology. They hold that the event of Jesus Christ somehow constitutes the possibility of salvation, which is nothing until this event occurs. But this contention that the Christ event is, in some way, the cause of salvation is open to a decisive objection.

This is the objection that, for any appropriate understanding of the Christ event, it is so far from being the cause of salvation as to be its consequence. The only cause of salvation, the argument goes, is the primordial and everlasting love of God, which is the sole primal source and the sole final end of anything that is so much as possible. Because of this love, which is nothing merely accidental in God but God's very essence, the same God who is the Creator and Consummator of all things is also the Savior of all men and women, as well as, presumably, of any other beings who, having misused their freedom, would likewise stand in need of salvation. But, then, no event in time and history, including the event of Jesus Christ, can be the cause of salvation in the sense of the necessary condition of its possibility. On the contrary, any event, including the Christ event, can be at most a consequence of the salvation, the sole necessary condition of the possibility of which is God's own essential being as all-embracing love.

Theologians who develop this argument commonly formulate it over against the so-called satisfaction theory of the atonement, according to which salvation becomes possible only because of the obedience of Jesus Christ, especially the passive obedience of his death on the cross. Thus Paul Tillich, for instance, rejects the claim that "in the Cross" salvation "becomes possible" on the ground that it necessarily implies that God "is the one who must be reconciled." Since the message of Christianity, on the contrary, is that "God, who is eternally reconciled, wants us to be reconciled to him," the only appropriate thing to say is that "through the Cross" salvation "becomes manifest" (Tillich 1957, 169f., 175f.). But, however the argument is developed, the objection to inclusivism is the same, and it clearly seems decisive. The Christ event cannot be the cause of salvation because its only cause, and the cause of this event itself, is the boundless love of God of which this event is the decisive re-presentation.

Not the least reason for being confident about this is that certain inclusivists themselves concede the decisiveness of the objection and go to great lengths to try to show why the constitutive christology they uphold is not vulnerable to it. This is particularly striking in the work of Karl Rahner, who entirely agrees that the saving event of Jesus Christ must be understood rather as the consequence than as the cause of God's universal will to save, at least if "cause" is understood in the usual sense of bringing about a physical or a moral change. Like the other theologians already mentioned, Rahner is especially critical in this connection of the satisfaction theory of the atonement on the ground that it "all but inevitably insinuates the idea of a fundamental change of mind in God, which is metaphysically impossible, and obscures the origin of the cross as a consequence of God's forgiving love" (Rahner, 262).

At the same time, Rahner accepts the traditional teaching according to which salvation is granted to men and women *intuitu meritorum Christi*—"in view of the merits of Christ" (263f.). Consequently, he is constrained to argue for a constitutive type of christology, which can understand the cross and the Christ event as a whole as being at least in some sense a cause with respect to salvation. The conceptuality he employs to do this involves, on the one hand, distinguishing between "efficient" and "final" causality and, on the other hand, elaborating an analogy between the kind of final causality proper to sacraments in general and the unique causality of the "primal sacrament" Jesus Christ. His thesis, then, is that, while the Christ event neither is nor can be the *efficient* cause of God's universal will to save, it is nonetheless the *final* cause of God's will, in that it is its definitive and irreversible sign and as such "the universal primal sacrament of the salvation of the whole world" (271).

Without claiming to offer an adequate criticism of Rahner's characteristically subtle and nuanced argument for this thesis, I can say that I find it by far the most ingenious defense of the constitutive type of christology underlying inclusivism of which I have any knowledge. If I were to be an inclusivist, it would be because his reasons for being one seemed to me to be good and sufficient reasons. But, as it is, I do not find his argument convincing. Despite his efforts, in effect, to avoid the choice between a constitutive and a representative type of christology, I do not see that he ever demonstrates a real, as distinct from a merely verbal, alternative. If there is a real and not merely a verbal difference in the Christ event's not being the efficient cause of God's saving will, but being its final cause instead, then, so far as I can see, the Christ event is not really constitutive of salvation after all, but only representative of it, similarly to the way in which sacraments in general are thus representative. If, on the contrary, the Christ event is different enough from sacraments generally not only to represent God's saving will but also to really constitute it, then, in my view, there is not a real, but only a verbal, difference in its being called the final cause of God's will to save instead of its efficient cause.

Therefore, my conclusion from Rahner's argument is that one can meet the decisive objection to the constitutive type of christology underlying inclusivism only by opting for a representative type of christology. But does this mean, then, that one can consistently think and speak of Jesus, not as savior, but merely as prophet, sage, or saint?

I do not believe so, despite the widespread assumption to the contrary on all sides of the usual discussion. Of course, if all that could be properly meant by Jesus' being savior is that he not only represents the possibility of salvation, but is also somehow constitutive of it, then one could not consistently think and speak of him as savior if one opted for a representative type of christology. But that one's only option, then, would be to think and speak of him merely as one more human being who bore witness to salvation or actualized it in his own life is

not so self-evidently true that one can simply assume it. On the contrary, there are good reasons for
rejecting it as false.

This should be clear enough from the analogy
already before us between the sacraments or means
of salvation and the event of Jesus Christ. This analogy is clearly suggested, it will be recalled, by
Robertson's statement that baptism is the revelation to an individual person of the same truth that
Christ revealed to the race—namely, that all, without exception, are already children of God de jure
by reason of their humanity. On the face of it, the
similarity that this analogy asserts is that the Christ
event, like baptism, is not constitutive of the possibility of salvation, but representative of it, while the
only difference it asserts is that baptism represents
this possibility particularly to the individual,
whereas Christ represents it universally to the
world. But this difference evidently implies the
further one, that baptism depends upon the Christ
event in a way in which the Christ event does not
depend upon baptism. In fact, we may say that the
Christ event is constitutive of baptism, whereas
baptism is only representative of the Christ event.
Thus, notwithstanding that baptism and the Christ
event are similar in that both represent the possibility of salvation but do not constitute it, they are also
significantly different in the ways in which they
represent this possibility.

Recognizing this, one can well appropriate the
conceptuality of Rahner and other inclusivists and
think and speak of the Christ event as the primal
Christian sacrament. In doing so, naturally, one

must deny any inclusivistic implication that this primal sacrament is somehow constitutive of the possibility of salvation itself. But there is no need to deny, and every reason to affirm, that the event of Jesus Christ *is* constitutive of the specifically Christian understanding of this possibility, and thus of all Christian sacraments and means of salvation as well as of the visible church and everything specifically Christian. For this reason, the Christ event cannot be thought and spoken of as *a* Christian sacrament, but only as *the* Christian sacrament, the one representation of the possibility of salvation upon which all other Christian representations of it, and Christian faith itself, are by their very nature dependent.

This means, however, that one not only cannot, but also need not, think and speak of Jesus merely as prophet, sage, or saint. One *can* not so think and speak of him because prophets, sages, and saints can never be constitutive of a faith or religion, in the way in which Jesus is constitutive of Christianity. In the nature of the case, they are always only one among others, dependent for their authority upon the explicit understanding of existence that alone is thus constitutive of the faith they represent. In the specific case of Christianity, however, this explicit understanding is not, in the first instance, some law or teaching or word of wisdom, but Jesus himself, through whom the meaning of ultimate reality for us is decisively re-presented. Consequently, the only way in which Jesus can be thought and spoken of consistently with his constitutive significance for the Christian religion is not as one more authority among others, even the first and foremost thereof, but as the primal authorizing source by which all Christian authorities, be they prophets, sages, or saints, are explicitly authorized as such.

But Jesus also *need* not be understood otherwise, since there is the obvious alternative of thinking and speaking of him with Rahner and others as the primal Christian sacrament. By "sacrament" here, of course, I mean what is better referred to more generally as "means of salvation." In my view, at any rate, sacraments in the ordinary sense are rightly thought of together with word as equivalent means of salvation in that they are equally valid ways of representing Jesus Christ as the explicit gift and demand of God's love. Thus it would be equally appropriate to develop an analogy between the word of preaching and Jesus and to think and speak of him, accordingly, as the primal Christian word, rather than as the primal Christian sacrament. In either case, the point of the analogy would be to assert both the similarity and the difference between ordinary means of salvation and Jesus Christ. Like both word and sacraments, he does not constitute God's love, but represents it. But whereas they represent God's love by also representing him, he represents God's love by also constituting them. Because this analogy is undoubtedly available, however, there is no need to think and speak of Jesus merely as prophet, sage, or saint. On the contrary, one can very well think and speak of him as savior, in the precise sense that, being the primal Christian word and sacrament, he has a significance for the specifically Christian religion and economy of salvation that is not merely representative but constitutive.

Even so, it is of the essence of the fourth option to insist that the possibility of salvation itself, as distinct from the specifically Christian representation of it, is constituted solely and sufficiently by God's primordial and everlasting love. This means, as I understand it, that, just as it is of the essence of God's love to create creatures and to consummate them by accepting them into God's own all-embracing life, so it is also essential to God's love to save sinners by being the necessary condition of the possibility of their salvation. I do not mean by this, naturally, that God could not exist as God without the existence of sinners needing salvation from the guilt and the power of sin. Even if it is necessary to God's existence ever to create and to consummate *some* creatures, no particular creature could be thus necessary to God and still be a creature in more than name only. Therefore, that sinners do in fact happen to exist is nothing necessary to God, but is as utterly contingent as is the fact that there happen to be beings for whom existence in the self-misunderstanding of sin is always a possibility. But once given God's creation of such beings and their misuse of their freedom to actualize this possibility, God must be their Savior as surely as God is their Creator and Consummator; for God *is* love, and there is no way for God to love sinners except to do all that could conceivably be done to save them from their sin. In this sense, the possibility of salvation that is decisively re-presented through Jesus Christ is always already constituted for each and every sinner by God's very being as love.

But if the Christian witness is true that it is just this love of God that is the strictly ultimate reality with which every human being has to do as soon and as long as she or he exists humanly at all, then not only Christianity but other religions as well can validly claim to be formally true. They can do so because all that is constitutive of the possibility of salvation and, therefore, also of any true religion is the boundless love of God that is and must be presented at least implicitly in every human existence. Provided, then, that a religious praxis is so transformed by God's love as to represent the possibility that it constitutes as our authentic self-understanding, it is, from a Christian standpoint, substantially true, and its claim to be formally true can be a valid claim, even if it is not the claim that Christians as such would have any reason to make.

Of course, to say that religions can validly claim to be formally true insofar as they explicitly represent God's love is a specifically Christian way of explaining this possibility. But to be a Christian and to take Christianity to be the formally true religion are one and the same thing. Every religion claims implicitly or explicitly to be formally true, and the adherents of any religion are bound to employ what it, in turn, specifies as formally normative as exactly that in judging all claims to religious truth. This need not mean, to be sure, that Christians today have to do this in the same dogmatic, uncritical way in which most religious believers have undoubtedly done it throughout the history of religion. There is the distinct alternative of recognizing the truth claim of the Christian religion to be exactly that—a claim—and of being willing to critically validate it through unrestricted dialogue and common